TIME'S BARTER

Haiku and Senryu

Kynpham

Sing Nongkynrih

HarperCollins *Publishers* India

First published in India in 2015 by
HarperCollins *Publishers* India

Building 10, Tower A, 4th Floor, DLF Cyber City, Phase II,
Gurugram Haryana - 122002, India
www.harpercollins.co.in

P-ISBN: 978-93-5029-863-3
E-ISBN: 978-93-5029-864-0

2 4 6 8 10 9 7 5 3 1

Typeset in 11/15 Scala at SURYA, New Delhi

Printed and bound at Microprints India, New Delhi

TIME'S BARTER

KYNPHAM SING NONGKYNRIH writes poems, short fiction and drama in Khasi and English. He has a total of thirteen publications in Khasi. His collections of poetry in English include *Moments, The Sieve* and *The Yearning of Seeds* (HarperCollins). He is the author of *Around the Hearth: Khasi Legends* (Penguin) and the co-editor of *Dancing Earth: An Anthology of Poetry from North-East India* (Penguin).

His poetry has been widely published in national and international journals, including *The New Welsh Review* (Cardiff); *Planet: The Welsh Internationalist* (Aberystwyth, Wales); *Karavan* (Stockholm); *PEN International* (London); *The Literary Review* (New Jersey); *Wasafiri* (London); *Modern Haiku* (Lincoln, USA); *Simply Haiku* (Pasadena, USA); *Poetry International Web* (Rotterdam); and *The Heron's Nest* (Nassau, USA).

His awards include the first Veer Shankar Shah-Raghunath Shah National Award for literature (Madhya Pradesh, 2008) and the first North-East Poetry Award (Tripura, 2004). He also received a Fellowship for Outstanding Artists from the Government of India in 2000.

*after Nigel's 'Gun',**
haiku fluttering as from
a subterranean cage.

**O for a Gun*, a collection of haiku and senryu by Nigel Jenkins.

ACKNOWLEDGEMENTS

My profound gratitude is due to Nigel Jenkins – award-winning Welsh poet, writer and critic – who read these haiku, offered invaluable suggestions and wrote the introduction. I'm additionally grateful to him for the inspiration that his collection of haiku, *O for a Gun*, has given me. Nigel passed away recently: 'May he take betel nut in the house of God,' as the Khasi saying goes.

My gratitude is also due to the following journals and anthologies, where some of these poems had first appeared: *Planet: The Welsh Internationalist* (Aberystwyth, Wales); *Simply Haiku* (Pasadena, USA); *Modern Haiku* (Lincoln, USA); *The Heron's Nest* (Nassau, USA); *Muse India* (Hyderabad); *Kavya Bharati* (Madurai); *The Shillong Times* (Shillong); *The Yearning of Seeds* (HarperCollins, New Delhi); *Dancing Earth: An Anthology of Poetry from North-East India* (Penguin, New Delhi); *Jabberwock* (New Delhi) and *The HarperCollins Book of English Poetry* (HarperCollins, New Delhi).

INTRODUCTION

This collection of haiku by Kynpham Sing Nongkynrih is in several respects a pioneering volume. The smallest of the world's literary forms, the haiku is best known, of course, in its birthplace, Japan, where it has been well established since at least the seventeenth century. But only fitfully, and in some places relatively recently, has the practice of haiku making spread beyond Japan.

The haiku may be the most popular form of poetry on the internet (a status not wholly to its advantage, given the deficiencies of many a net-borne 'haiku'), but there are still many parts of the world where it has yet to make itself at home as a form successfully adapting itself to indigenous cultural conditions, so that it may be counted as an unquestioned part of a country's literary landscape – in the same way that, say, the originally Italian sonnet became wholly naturalized in the literature of England and other countries. All too often, the haiku is either wilfully misunderstood or disdained and dismissed as an alien and pointless fey trifle of a thing.

This book represents a breakthrough for the haiku not only in the north-east of India, where, I gather from anthologists of the region's literature, there are no known haiku practitioners, but also in India as a whole, where there may be little more than half a dozen serious haiku poets and where few significant 'mainstream'[1] poets have expressed any interest in the form. It is a breakthrough, furthermore, for the author, who until now has been known as a 'mainstream' poet (as well as a short-story writer, translator, editor and anthologist):

late-blooming cherries
by the highway—how else can I
describe my haiku?

If, as his prefatory poem suggests, my own haiku have helped nurture Kynpham's 'late blooming', I am delighted to have been something of a catalyst, although the credit for his considerable achievement rests entirely

---

[1]The term 'mainstream poet' is used commonly among haiku poets to denote those who write in other, longer forms.

with him. Additionally gratifying is the fact that the connection between our two literary 'projects' owes much, indirectly, to an old, imperial association between our two countries: from 1841 until the 1960s, Presbyterian missionaries from my native Wales were an influential presence in Kynpham's Khasi Jaiñtia Hills, in what is now the state of Meghalaya. Theirs was a typical colonialist mission field, and the effects on Khasi culture of their strict Calvinistic outlook were not always beneficial. But the Welsh in the Khasi Jaiñtia Hills are generally given credit, by Christians and non-Christians alike, for championing the Khasi language and for laying the foundations for its written literature. It was in the early 1990s, while researching this fascinating but then little-known chapter of Welsh history, that I met Kynpham and some of the other leading writers of the Hills; since then, we have had the pleasure of developing the old association between our two lands on a more secular and, in particular, cultural level.

India, of course, is a vastly bigger country than Wales, but its experience of the haiku is in some ways comparable to that of Wales; I hope, therefore, that readers will bear with me in this introduction if sometimes I invoke Wales's negotiation of the haiku to illustrate a point or two that might also apply to the development of the haiku in India.

Because few 'mainstream' literary magazines are hospitable to the haiku, most haiku tend to be published in specialist – and therefore somewhat ghettoized – outlets. A successful haiku may surely be enjoyed by any reader, even without the benefit of background knowledge, but there's no doubt that, as with any art, some understanding of the haiku's purpose and ways of working will greatly enrich a reader's experience of the form. A few explanatory remarks about this specialized and often misrepresented mode of writing might therefore prove helpful – particularly to new readers.

Ask almost any graduate of junior school what they know about the haiku, and they will invariably reply that it's a short Japanese poem of three lines, with five syllables in the first line, seven in the second, and five in the third – and that is usually the extent of their 'knowledge'. Even 'mainstream' poets frequently demonstrate, in the half dozen alleged haiku they might publish in their collections, that their understanding of the form has advanced little since they 'did' the haiku in school. There is, of course, much more to the haiku than mere syllable counts; in concerning ourselves too much with the haiku's outward form, we risk losing sight of its essence.

In Japan, the haiku – meaning, literally, 'pleasure verse' – is a popular and enduring form, appealing to people from all walks of life, and rousing considerable passions among the numerous movements and factions that have developed around competing interpretations of the haiku's role and aesthetics. It has a long history and – like, say, the (generally) four-line Welsh englyn or the sonnet – it did not spring suddenly into fixed and immutable shape, but evolved from an antecedent form, and continues to evolve. The Japanese have been composing around a 5-7-5 matrix from at least as early as the eighth century. By the fifteenth, the *haikai-no-renga*, linked verses of seventeen 'syllables', had become popular, and innovators began detaching the *hokku*, or 'starting verse', from the *renga* – which could be anything from thirty-six to a thousand stanzas long – and tendering it as an 'unfinished' but sufficient poem in itself. The work of early haiku masters such as Bashô (1644-94), Buson (1716-84) and Issa (1762-1826) reflects, of course, a pre-industrial world; it may be, still, that the haiku lives most fully in nature, for whatever its subject it never allows us to forget that we, no less than that spider or this droplet of water, are part of the living cosmos. But it also reflects a changing world: the haiku developed as the art of a burgeoning, but initially despised and powerless, merchant class, disdainful of tradition and fixed on the moment. Continuing to reflect social and cultural changes, the haiku has moved effortlessly into the street, the factory, the office, the airport, and may cast its wise, forgiving eye on almost any aspect of modern life. If Kynpham's haiku and senryu[2] instinctively celebrate the natural life and culture of his native hills, they are also avowedly of his times, with frequent references to things such as traffic jams, timber trucks, elections, emails and mobile telephones, and to pressing contemporary phenomena such as poverty, over-population and global warming.

Although he has written much in his native language, Khasi, he has chosen to make his haiku in English, which has been a medium for the haiku, in certain parts of the world, for the best part of a century. Its

[2]Senryu: a form of haiku that foregrounds humour and/or social observation.

influence can be felt in the work of 'mainstream' American poets such as Wallace Stevens (1879–1955; see, for instance, his 'Thirteen Ways of Looking at a Blackbird'), Ezra Pound (1885–1972) and William Carlos Williams (1883–1963); without the energies of the haiku, Williams would probably have seen his red wheelbarrow, his plums and his locust tree rather differently. It was American Beat Poets such as Jack Kerouac (1922–69), Allen Ginsberg (1926–97) and Gary Snyder (1930), intimately conversant with Zen Buddhism, who were primarily responsible, from the 1950s onwards, for launching the haiku on its Western career – not that the haiku should be considered as always interpreting life from a Zen point of view (although the characteristics of Zen art – asymmetry, simplicity, freedom, naturalness, profundity, unworldliness, stillness – may recommend themselves to many a non-Zen artist). The challenge for non-Japanese haiku poets is to find ways of refracting the haiku form through the valencies of their own languages and cultures, respecting the poem's original animus while eschewing pseudo-Japanese moods and effects.

Many of the pioneers of the English-language haiku were stimulated by the Beats-influenced literary climate of the 1960s, although they were often experimenting with this novel form in isolation. One such was the distinguished poet, translator and critic Tony Conran, who was editing the seminally important *Penguin Book of Welsh Verse* (1967) at about the same time as he was penning the first haiku to be written (in either Welsh or English) in Wales. The haiku, he felt, answered a need of the time: 'The sixties in general tried to cut themselves off from history except as a kind of flavour. The emphasis was on nowness, as in adverts or pin-ups. The haiku's isolation of the given moment as opposed to a continuous passage of constructed consciousness, as well as its minimalism (its 'slenderness'), had great appeal.'[3]

The small-press scene in Britain and the United States, with its 'alternative' inclinations and built-in Zen enthusiasms, was considerably more receptive to the haiku (or what purported to be haiku) than most mainstream or 'establishment' outlets, although much of what passed for haiku in Britain until about 1990 fell somewhat wide of the mark.

---

[3]From Tony Conran's unpublished essay 'Haiku as an English poetic form: a personal approach'.

The 1970 to 1990 period in Wales, as in Britain generally, seemed to generate little haiku activity, with mainstream poets tending to dismiss the haiku as some faddy hangover from the 1960s – if, indeed, they paid it any regard at all. But since about 1990, the haiku pace has perceptibly quickened. The founding in that year of the British Haiku Society[4] gave haiku enthusiasts their first opportunity to meet each other, and to debate, publish and promote a literary form whose development in the countries of Britain had been impeded by the isolation of its practitioners and by the lack of consensus as to what, in British and European terms (rather than according to the dominant American view), might constitute a functioning haiku on the western Atlantic seaboard. Respecting the integrity of the nations and regions of Britain, the BHS has sought to foster not 'the British haiku' (perish the grotesque thought) but a theory and practice appropriate to the making of haiku wherever in these islands poets find themselves working. Although some sort of definitional consensus – which pays proper regard to Japanese essentials while acknowledging the need to adapt the form to indigenous

[4]By the English haikuists David Cobb (1926) and Dee Evetts (1943).

conditions – seems by now to have been reached, vigorous debate continues on many related issues, with national and regional branches flying the flag for local particularity and diversity. Perhaps the time is ripe in India for a comparable discussion among poets as to what might be agreed upon as to the role(s) and characteristics of the haiku in a specifically Indian context.

An early bone of contention in such discussions has usually concerned the status of the syllable count. Many of Kynpham's haiku conform to the 5-7-5 syllable count that used to be considered obligatory; but some, unashamedly, do not. To appear to stray from the 5-7-5 'rule' – and the Japanese themselves were the first to do so, nearly a hundred years ago – is less controversial than it used to be, as it has become better understood that a mechanical replication of Japanese formal conditions is not necessarily the most subtle means of equipping the haiku in a non-Japanese context. The Japanese haiku is, of course, an organic outgrowth of the language itself, and the 5-7-5 rhythm in Japanese haiku is not the matter of arbitrary choice that it may appear to be to a non-Japanese writer. Various combinations of five and seven syllables have dominated the Japanese literary scene for most of its history – tanka[5] and haiku being the most prominent examples. To most Japanese, words phrased in these configurations have a remarkably mnemonic quality, so much so that much war and political propaganda has exploited the form; a comparable mnemonic quality in an English haiku might be more readily achieved from a patterning of accented syllables. Furthermore, where the English language owes much of its grammatical simplicity to the fact that word order plays a major role in determining the relationships between words and phrases – which cannot be moved about freely without changing the meaning of a sentence – the Japanese language is grammatically far more malleable, and thus easier to fit into a rigid form such as 5-7-5. In languages such as English, whose grammar is heavily dependent on word order, haiku may work better by departing from certain aspects of the Japanese form.

To talk in terms of 'syllables' and horizontal 'lines' is in any case misleading. A traditional Japanese haiku

[5]Tanka: a five-line poem, predating the haiku, which tends to focus on love and nature.

appears on the page, often in association with a painting or drawing, as a single vertical line, albeit divisible into three phrases. The word translated as 'syllable' is 'onji', but, strictly, 'onji' doesn't mean 'syllable', it means 'sound symbol', and these sound symbols are shorter than an English syllable – perhaps somewhere between a phoneme and a syllable. It is generally understood now that approximately twelve English syllables best duplicate the traditional Japanese seventeen-*onji* haiku – an utterance that should be expressible in one emission of breath. Since Anglophone poets started writing haiku, adopting fairly uncritically the 5-7-5 pattern, there has grown an awareness that seventeen English syllables convey a great deal more information than seventeen Japanese *onji*; many haiku poets have come to write haiku – and translate Japanese haiku – in fewer syllables, while others are content to vary their approach, even permitting themselves the occasional indulgence of a syllable or two beyond the holy seventeen. The haiku's brevity is nevertheless one of its essential characteristics. As Harold Henderson has remarked, 'Haiku is more akin to silence than to words,' an observation which relates to the famous, and sometimes almost minimalist, 'suggestiveness' of the form: Japanese artists influenced by Zen, believing that 'more is less', have tended to use the fewest possible words or strokes of the brush to suggest a whole world of experience: therefore, the shorter an English-language haiku, (generally) the better. Although some haiku have been translated in a four-line format, and some are written as one- or two-liners, most retain a three-line shape, with the second a little longer than the other two, producing an irregular two-three-two rhythm, without rhyme. 'The division into three gives us the feeling of ascent, attainment, and resolution of experience,' wrote R.H. Blyth (1898-1964), the great English interpreter of Japanese poetry. 'The haiku form is thus a simple and yet deeply "natural" form, compared to the sonnet, blank verse, and other borrowed forms of verse in English.'

There is debate, too, about other aspects of the haiku which traditionalists would deem formal requirements: the presence, for instance, of the *kireji*, or 'cutting word', which is often best answered for in English by a dash or comma; and the importance of a clear reference to season, if not, indeed, time of day. Such matters are not irrelevant, but to obsess ourselves with them at the expense of the actual poetry of the haiku is to drift into the folly of the sound-system enthusiast who is more interested in his equipment than in the music it makes.

'Haiku,' said Bashô, stressing the importance of intuitive experience, 'is simply what is happening in this place, at this moment.' Not a form for philosophical, religious or political generalizations and abstractions, the haiku is intensely attentive to particular times, places and situations, as mediated through the unique sensibility of the individual haikuist. The haiku moment may be personal – indeed, self-portraiture is one of the haiku's dominant modes:

in the looking glass
this morning—a man who hates
my mid-aged face.

– but it is never private, requiring a key to crack a code, nor is it a riddle. It is an act of sharing that finds completion only when its words come into contact with the imagination of a reader – who, in Bill Wyatt's words, supplies the match that sets the haiku tinder aflame.

It is brief and precise, yet mysterious; it is direct and simple, yet as capable as a koan of embodying enigma, paradox, obliquity. Its language is down-to-earth and colloquial:

potato flowers!
no one sees, only thinking
of the fat root within.

– for it is a sensory form, using concrete imagery to express emotion and, often, a sense of terrestrial and cosmic wonderment. Bashô suggested that traditional courtly poetry – against which the haiku rebelled – was like the fragrance of the plum tree, whereas the haiku resembled the roughness of the pine tree. The haiku encourages us to make distinctions and enjoy contrasts: to appreciate the little, neglected, 'irrelevant' things we routinely edit out of our busy lives as unimportant – what Wordsworth called 'seeing into the life of things' – as well as directing us towards the ineffable sweep of the night sky and the awesome interior spaces of the atom.

It cultivates the Zen ideal of according an object the kind of attention that enables us not so much to look *at* it but to look *as* it – or to commune directly with it, as co-participant in the wonder of existence:

creepy caterpillar,
when did you become
these flying colours?

While directness, simplicity and observational accuracy are essential, self-conscious literary embellishment is held to be a distraction, drawing attention more to the writerly skills of the haiku-maker than to the object or moment of the haiku itself: the 'spiderness' of the spider is what the haiku invites us to consider, not the author's esteemed ability to write about spiders. Simile, therefore, is rare; so too, it is often claimed, is metaphor – but this is not really the case: there is no shortage of metaphor in haiku, but haiku metaphors are notably oblique and unostentatious (although often highly charged with emotion), as indeed the metaphors in Kynpham's haiku are. It may be useful, initially, to describe a haiku as 'a word photograph', but that ultimately insufficient definition reduces the haiku's function to the mere imagistic recording of surfaces. The haiku is much more exploratory than a 'word photograph', and is profoundly engaged with depth, resonance and transformation, being, in Martin Lucas's words, an 'open metaphor' for the human condition. An unsuccessful haiku fails, frequently, because it is merely descriptive of a scene or moment, and has not been invested with that difficult-to-define, elusive entity, resonance.

Another significant feature of the haiku is its understated humour. The senryu is derived from the name of Karai Senryu (1718-90), a poet who was an anthologist interested in collecting poems of wit and irony. Writers and readers with a more satirical sensibility sometimes prefer the senryu to the haiku, although it is not always easy to tell them apart. The senryu has the same formal characteristics as the haiku, but tends to display a greater interest in human relations. 'The aim of senryu,' wrote R.H. Blyth, 'is to bring out into the open the sentimentality, affectation, swindling, and hypocrisy in the world; to expose the unobserved or purposely overlooked contradiction in what men say and what they actually do; to lay bare all the hidden motives, the secret shames, the useless wisdom, and foolish misery of mankind.'

Kynpham's haiku and senryu abound with humour, in a range of registers, from wry (and sometimes simultaneously sad) vignettes of married life:

wind by bedside window—
all covers are blown,
exposed to my wife.

to knowing asides on the process of ageing:

black shirt with grey lines—
an ageing man wears
the colour of his hair.

– to the laugh-aloud comedy of the partially 'found poem':

region's backwardness
explained by a road sign:
'slow men at work'

– or

fish tale—common carp
by Umiam Lake, bought, then caught,
by city anglers.

But, in the accepting, generous spirit of haiku, his humour is never harsh and rarely judgemental:

prostitute's kindness:
'Come home with me, something is
better than nothing.'

His gaze, though, is open and unflinching, no matter how horrific the matter:

city's cluttered drains—
even unwanted infants
are often thrown in.

At their best, these haiku – full of rain, clouds, plums and (like the Japanese) cherries, domestic life, city vistas and unclichéd vignettes of the abundant nature for which his land is renowned – richly exemplify the three defining features which Tony Conran has isolated as the essence of haiku: 'loneliness, tenderness and slenderness'. Then there are the characteristic attributes of brevity, concision, simplicity, presence, sensory directness and present-tense immediacy. There's a quality of profound attention, often to minutiae, and a sharpness of observation mediated by down-to-earth, unembellished language.

The quality of his haiku writing has already been recognized in Wales, where the leading cultural magazine *Planet: the Welsh Internationalist* has recently published in its pages a selection of his haiku. One looks forward, now, to seeing what ripples they might make on the still youthful haiku scene of India.

NIGEL JENKINS
formerly of the University of Swansea, Wales

juicy-looking plums,
watery taste—shouldn't have
plucked on a rainy day.

wind-whipping rain—
on the soggy earth,
blood-red, the plums.

dark foreboding sky—
scarlet plums,
festive with bulbuls.

succulent plums,
the flesh fragrant and sweet—
sour at the core.

paramour rain—
at the bedroom window,
spousy wind screaming.

drizzly afternoon,
wife yawns:
'Feels like a nap again?'

rainwater gurgling
gaily in the gutter—
how can I run so low?

land clouds seeping
through pine trees—
a will-o'-the-wisp.

sluggish drain flow—
city folk
going to office.

monsoon runnels on hill slopes—
city folk
rushing from office.

in the looking glass
this morning—a man who hates
my mid-aged face.

a couple kissing
in the park—sickening
this sour grape.

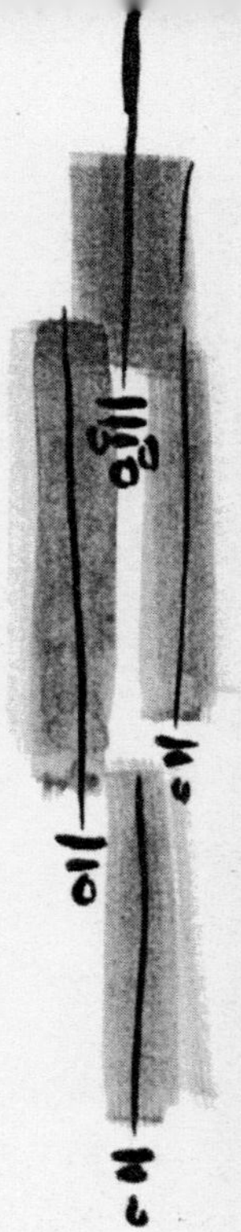

facial?
skin needs
ironing.

someone's at the door—
wind
jingling wind chimes.

puffy eyes,
large crow's feet—
face it like an old man.

dipping a finger
in water—that's making love
with her.

waiting at 'Barbers'—
an ageing man, know not for what,
takes forever.

driving in the rain—
streets empty and peaceful:
wish every day were Sunday.

early morning's most
unpoetic sound—the scandal
of bathroom fans.

yellow, red and green—
the pennant of
ripening cherries.

while the rain keeps us
from work, a black and white bird
pecks at black cherries.

rain for days—
only soldiers' clothes flapping
on a sagging line.

nine days of rain:
what use the crowing
of a cockerel?

mizzly afternoon:
the relay calls of roosters,
and then, a rainbow.

green pears on green leaves—
simply-clad village girl,
inherently lovely.

creepy caterpillar,
when did you become
these flying colours?

wife's promotion and transfer—
life's
bitter-sweet-bitter things...

midsummer night—
the moon, a snake boat
fishing stars.

deep forest—
columns of charcoal smoke
hazing the sky.

Cherra's deep jungle—
a thunderous river raging,
a living root bridge.

autumn sky spreading
heaps of cotton wool—all set
to make winter rugs.

effervescent milk
filling a deep gorge—
Likai Falls in summer.

at forty-three
even a slight smile is hostile
to my youthful looks.

pears, plums, black cherries:
for how long, when iron rods
are pointing at the sky?

fresh green leaves atop
an orange tree—white atop
my head, also fresh.

self-authored volume
newly arrived—I begin by
smelling the stories.

green soldiers
stripping the hillside bare—
grass caterpillars gorging.

last haiku of Bashõ—
alone
facing a blank page.

land clouds rising—
certainly, smoke
without fire.

foggy morning—
how blessed just once not to see
the barracks opposite.

how hopeful to watch
hip-hops with falling pants
doing traditional dance.

squash
growing overnight—
greedy eyes inspecting.

bad neighbour's squash,
their tentacles over the wall
reach out for a handshake.

winter fog—
even a dragonfly
wants to come inside.

dawn—
garlic-skin moon
palely sinking.

wet desert's wilderness—
Cherra,*
inhospitably lovely.

---

*Sohra or Cherrapunjee, the wettest place on earth.

winding road by a river—
jingling church bells?
a smithy.

heating, hit; dipping, hit—
iron, shaped by fire,
shaped by water.

never knew bulbuls
feeding at dawn, noisy as
Khasi funerals.

rule-the-roost gridlock—
cars don't have a death rate,
only birth.

aroma of brewing tea—
dawn?
Village Defence (midnight) Party.

drizzling in the sun—
at the end of a rainbow,
a filthy stream.

fat leeches sucking
a man
with puffy under-eyes.

white rosacea blooms
above bottle-green leaves—
flowers in the crown.

dawn alive with birds
and roosters; morning, raucous
with cackling females.

stark embarrassment—
a footpath vendor measures
bras for a blushing girl.

uprooted natives—
orchids hawked
on city pavements.

a rainbow straddling hills:
suddenly, from where this vague
expectant feeling?

viewing sunset—
a girl with projecting mounds
sets the sky on fire.

sunset behind a tree—
the mystery
of the burning bush.

a friend failing
in the city—happiness
coming home.

hometown's visit—
treasures misplaced since childhood
at last recovered.

fiery pomegranate
bursting with ripe seeds—earth
bursting with humans.

layered clouds—
earth fractured
by long drought.

dog baying all night—
shouldn't be tied when the rest
are out bitching.

canine love-making—
more ashamed he who looks
than he who craps.

wind by bedside window—
all covers are blown,
exposed to my wife.

of all the days in a year
why should this meeting fall
on my wife's birthday?

wind among rain clouds—
herdsmen on the road, driving
cows to a slaughter hill.

monsoon—
naked boys fishing
among green lotuses.

momos steaming in a jar:
people inside cars
in a Delhi summer.

yearning—
so many days without hills
in the metropolis.

after lorries,
highway cattle
cause a gridlock.

region's backwardness
explained by a road sign:
'slow men at work'.

fish tale—common carp
by Umiam Lake, bought, then caught,
by city anglers.

long-absent husband
finally calls his wife:
'How is the cat now?'

crookedness—
a human and a snake
never run straight.

women scanning fish
on strings—how can dead bodies
be so appealing?

fortunate mismatch—
wife
not reading poems.

wind chimes tinkling—
how sweetly, when she calls,
the telephone rings.

bamboo shoots pointing
to the sky—old bamboo trunks,
heads bent to the ground.

windy night—
feverish
till sunrise.

mother berating—
lightning flashes,
her lashing tongue.

pineapples piled
on the roadside—the pity
of rotting plenty.

daughter's birthday:
a 'death day'?
neither cakes nor greetings.

blustery evenings—
cold fed unendingly
on sneezes.

wind clamouring—
a drunk on the roadside
won't let me sleep all night.

that blue light behind
dark clouds, whose world, luminous
above this night gloom?

evening on a hill—
even the sun can be cupped
in these tiny palms.

autumn leaves falling—
time's barter, dreadful
for humans alone.

mother labours
up and down a coal mine—children
feasting on white rice.

unopened email—
your dark name alone
glowing white.

deep summer—
every clothesline overrun
by clambering squash.

such exquisite greens
in the forest, such ugly
distinctions among us.

forest fire watched
by millions; fire in my heart
witnessed by no one.

woman power—
I have forgotten to remember
to forget you.

Shillong infection—
even child beggars are busy
chewing betel-nuts.

riots in Shillong—
the police, dog's bark harmful
to communal peace.

queuing for gas:
how unsightly we all are
in the morning!

a heathen's rooster *
on top of All Saints' Cathedral?
only a weathercock.

---

*Symbol of Khasi indigenous faith.

moon of gold rising:
not even a dark haze can spoil
life's rare loveliness.

Ri Bhoi pineapples—
the car, fragrant
with a friend's gift.

prostitute's kindness:
'Come home with me, something is
better than nothing'.

long line of houses
up the woods of Shillong Peak—
a spear thrust through the heart.

black shirt with grey lines—
an ageing man wears
the colour of his hair.

life's paradoxes—
most precious, most abhorrent:
the yellow of gold and crap.

drunken man
left face down on the street—
a sick man dying.

Idols of the Age,
born of mere children
with voting cell phones.

promise-fertile friend—
meat dripping fat when roasted,
tough when ingested.

bee on a rain-wet floor—
after saving the bee, how
can I eat the cow?

five-day-night deluge—
only arum leaves not wet;
gathering crystals.

nature's loyal friends—
down-to-earth rural folk, their
huts made of mud.

one year to fresh polls:
summer wind brings noises of
bitter mudslinging.

night, how should I know,
daughters at twelve have also
seen their first red moon?

girl with bold praises—
an electric switch turning
a grey-haired's heater on.

cold twilight shower—
bulbuls
hunched on maize stalks.

why shouldn't I love these
bulbuls on the plums? their songs
are for free.

cold winter downpour:
daughters driven to school see their
father's sudden worth.

cherries in winter!
not everyone likes
globalization.

pink cherry blossoms
are now a jaded green;
winter, a jaded grey.

when winter cherries
go, what shall I write about?
black flies mass-mating.

mass-mating black flies
dying while lovemaking—
what more can one ask?

New Year's sunny day—
girls on the road, flowering;
wintering, I mope.

frosty winter fog—
even my favourite girlfriend
has put on the chills.

ripe areca-nuts
on my sofa? mid-ager
with a head on fire.

seeping wintry mist—
sweet companions, what is this
seeping into our lives?

peeling bananas:
with great love, I peel the skin
off Bashõ's haiku.

gliding dragonfly—
from such heights leaders too view
scenes of daily life.

farmer engrossed with
cauliflowers; couldn't even
see blooming cherries.

winter solitude?
blasts of the festive season
ringing in my ears.

village moon,
comes too early—so too
the early-pregnant girls.

white moon against white sky—
why is white on our heads
never as beautiful?

warblers on the pears—
how colourfully lovely,
crapping with a squirt!

December afternoon:
an old man half-bent with age?
a shivering youth.

winter's arrival:
it darts from the pines, licking
with an icy tongue.

twilight scene:
darkness does not fall from the sky,
it creeps along the ground.

late-blooming cherries
by the highway—how else can I
describe my haiku?

overturned highway
lorries—overfed autumn
beetles on their backs.

tree stumps on a hill,
opposite, in a ditch,
a laden timber truck.

plum blooming in the dead
of winter! his gaze rapt on
a lovely girl tenant.

bright winter morning—
clouds around the hills, all set
to draw the curtains.

white moon on low hills—
escort rider en route for
militant Imphal.

New Year's Eve midnight—
a half-moon hanging low, bares
its buttocks at the din.

very first New Year's Day,
as Old Year's very last:
gloomy, windy, cold.

tomato plants round
a plum tree—my hands gory
with their green blood.

January blooms—
an apricot tree in white,
a girl by its side.

plum blossoms—
if only I could rove with these
many-kindred bees!

golden bee
sprawled on snowy plum petals:
this is all it needs.

plums emerging in
winter? not only girls
are carrying early.

low tree laden
with star fruits—spring dancers
laden with gold pendants.

a whiff of bay leaf—
suddenly mother's kitchen
fragrant with lentils.

ripe star fruits
on drooping branches—
our greed knows no bounds.

classless society—
professor and mechanics,
whisky and grilled pork.

'No-Right-Turn' sign:
a car with a red light
turns right.

state's coldest place:
the morning road a black thread
into blinding fog.

only in Cherra
can the sunset offer
a blood-red plum.

budding pineapples—
even fruits
have ugly ducklings.

yellow of lemons,
dearer than the yellow of gold
to weary trekkers.

warm spring wind!
the house yellow with
sticky pine pollen.

dense smoke from pine copse—
man's baleful fire hell-bent
on quick destruction.

potato flowers!
no one sees, only thinking
of the fat root within.

moonless night:
the yard flickering
with glow-worms.

worm in an acorn:
drilled in by an awl?
a crafty parent.

first spring rain—
the bus-shelter
only half-finished.

early morning frost—
an old man washing nappies
by a water tank.

jacaranda blooms—
for weeks haven't been able
to stand and stare.

taking a midday nap,
the banter of house builders
wakens my conscience.

wind, rain and fog:
the car crawls
to a Cherra welcome.

foggy afternoon:
my wife nearby,
a bodiless soul.

picture-imperfect—
a golden butterfly perched
on a pile of poop.

bonfire evening—
all the songs,
from my youth.

rain flooding streets—
her love,
flooding my lifeblood.

summer spectacle—
rain comes thundering,
everyone scrambles in.

a distant crowd cheering!
rain from out of town,
slowly approaching.

autumn moon,
silvery on a mountain
of broken concrete.

dawn, loud with warblers—
how maddening,
after a sleepless night.

trees planted—
a blue-winged butterfly
perches on my arm.

stunning sunset—
a deciduous sacred grove,
frozen in amber.

from dark clouds
to a dark forest—
a rainbow.

village road—
a naked boy in the rain,
holding an umbrella.

a fly trying to leave
by a window pane—
half the day is lost.

follow the leader—
baby caterpillars
in a procession.

love marriage—
the son-in-law as bald as
the father-in-law.

plane touching down—
the city's buildings,
a vast pile of litter.

humid evening—
the mosquitoes more drawn
to sex than my blood.

early autumn—
rutting dogs make the streets
embarrassing.

Stupas of Sanchi—
a monk under a tree, lost
in a mobile phone.

thorny acorn
with velvety interior—
a safe and snug home.

annual cleaning drive—
garbage from the drains
piled onto roadsides

bolted shaman's door—
the mystical world
is closed for today.

deep forest—
by the highway,
neat stacks of timber.

broomstick country—
nothing grows
but broomsticks.

jungle road—
bay leaves fragrant
from gunnysacks.

agrarian villages—
on precipitous slopes,
slashed jungle burns.

autumn hailstorm—
the streets a thick carpet
of russet pine leaves.

state's cleanest village—
a white azalea bloom
in the jungle.

houses by a cemetery—
the dead are afraid
of the living.

winter shower—
the aroma
of cooked earth.

thorny trees—
how helpless against the saws
of Neemrana women!

Jaipur afternoon—
three girls on a pavement bent
on their homework.

Kolkata toilets—
in a ladies' booth, a cobbler
mending soles.

summer evening:
beetles, ladybirds and white ants,
my reading buddies.

summer afternoon—
white ants from their holes,
birds on the wing.

clammy summer night—
there's a lady in my bed,
a ladybird.

bookmaker's counter—
gods of all faiths bless
from the walls.

incessant downpour—
the noise of bulbuls: are they
singing or wailing?

Umïam Viewpoint—
heaps of rubbish
at my feet.

radiant dawn—
her eyes,
lightening the day.

radiant dawn—
her eyes,
aglow with sunrise.

wild yellow petal—
on its fragrant pollen bed,
beetles making love.

highway temptation:
'cold beer
sold here'.

in a crack
on the new concrete wall—
a single flower.

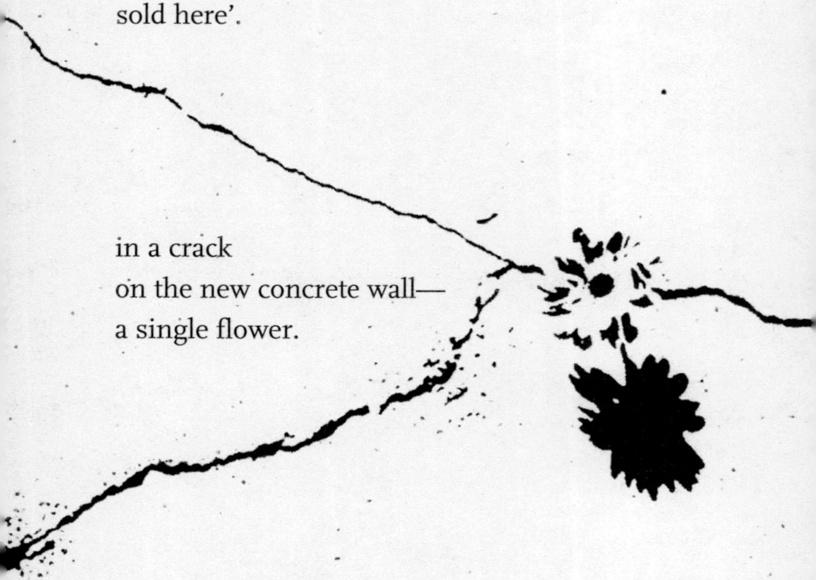

swirling cherry petals:
my mind swirling
with thoughts of you.

wet summer morning—
the dull grey of the clouds is
also in my brain.

morning drive:
a man peeing on a wall,
a dog on a post.

green caterpillar,
though lovely, you cannot feed
on the orange tree.

fresh sign of ageing—
bending down,
an ordeal.

rutting dogs mobbing
a single bitch—nowadays,
a familiar craze.

verdant summer:
in the yard an orange tree,
yellowing.

where all the cars of
Sunday worshippers are parked—
a no-parking zone.

roadside monkeys—
a woman, picking lice
from her son's head.

Fisheries' Office—
the fishponds by its side,
completely dry.

deep winter—
a mosquito,
still buzzing for blood.

market scene—
vegetables on footpaths,
shoes on glass cases.

calendar on the wall—
for a year at least I can look
before and after.

Cherra monsoon—
the deep gorges evened out
by land clouds.

Cherra monsoon—
hills foamy
with waterfalls.

pastoral landscape—
above a dense sacred grove,
huge sprawling buildings.

progress—
the hills will flatten
because of you.

on a projector
high above a classroom—
a bird's nest.

calling my dead mother's
cell phone, a message says:
'No communication methods.'

drone on a flower!
isn't sex
his full-time job?

electrified village—
more illumined by lightning
than electricity.

sundown—
a tree in the courtyard
folds its leaves.

SHILLONG IN HAIKU

Shillong's hot debate—
is it a town? a city?
Scotland of the East.

Scotland of the East—
roads pockmarked by jumbo pits,
cars do twist dancing.

cars over potholes—
gut-jerking see-saw, always
full of expletives.

chock-a-block traffic—
driving through the city streets:
stampeding wild beasts.

liberal police,
traffic run by
passenger-mad cabbies.

cars through crowded streets,
maximum rate per hour—
caterpillar speed.

locality roads,
linking each one to the city—
wide, as kettle necks.

Scotland of the East—
teeming, disorderly streets
fragrant with garbage.

survival technique—
woman gorging with dogs from
brimful garbage dump.

Ïew Mawlong Market—
vehicles plough through mud fields,
crowd scales rubbish heaps.

famed Umkhrah River—
reeking serpent of sewage,
bodies and drowned gods.

city's many streams
gushing from wooded catchments—
all drains lead to them.

city's cluttered drains—
even unwanted infants
are often thrown in.

Queen of Hill Stations—
flies swarming hearts, lungs, entrails,
dangling from meat shops.

Scotland of the East—
favourite architecture,
squat concrete boxes.

city's preferred paint—
grey lichen and dark monsoon
fungus with green moss.

chaotic city—
footpaths, overbridges are
favoured shopping malls.

Scotland of the East,
suitably provided with
its very own wonders.

Ïewduh Flyover:*
hanging garden of the world's
second-hand garments.

Crow Borough Hotel:
a government dream project,
for decades, a dream.

*Pulled down in September 2014 after it was declared unsafe.

multi-lane by-pass:
amazingly by-passing
construction for years.

public health centres:
mooing and baaing noises,
oh, livestock shelters!

Central Library—
the emptiness of shelves is
educational.

end of hot debate—
Shillong, a town? a city?
Scotland of the East.

GESTURES

man telling a tale—
a loud tune, friend turns away,
left hand holding his ear.

cute girl on the road,
left hand on left ear, looking
at me says, ‘Shut up!’

lone woman strolling by,
left hand on left ear, and then,
to the air, 'But where?'

young man ambling along,
left hand holding left ear, smiles
and smiles at no one.

man sitting with friends,
a song, left hand grabs left ear,
jumps to a corner.

lady by a lane,
hand on left ear, suddenly
thumps the air: 'Yahoo!'

lone girl with long hair,
right hand on right ear, briskly
nodding at the ground.

man at a workshop,
a hum, gets up, hand on his ear,
turns his back on all.

lady in a meeting,
a squeak, grabs her ear, her head
beneath the table.

girl clutching her left ear,
finger raised, eyes blazing, lips
flapping angrily.

newly discovered
contagion of modern age—
ear clutching itch.